Longing
Distance

L O N

T P

TUPELO PRESS

D I S T

G I N G

Sarah Hannah

A N C E

First paperback edition
Library of Congress Control Number: 2003115524
Tupelo Press
PO Box 539, Dorset, Vermont 05251
802.366.8185 • Fax 802.362.1883
editor@tupelopress.org • web www.tupelopress.org

On the cover:
A Beautiful Trifid, National Optical Asronomy Observatory,
950 North Cherry Avenue, Tucson, AZ 85719-4933

Cover and text designed by William Kuch, WK Graphic Design

For Bob, with love, curbside—

ACKNOWLEDGMENTS

The author gratefully acknowledges the editors of the following publications, in which some of the poems herein first appeared, some in slightly different form:

Barrow Street: "Cassetta Frame (Italy, circa 1600)," "The Dark Bookcases," "Lethe"

Boulevard: "The Linen Closet"

Crab Orchard Review: "'Sally Go Round the Roses'"

Gulf Coast: "Eclipse"

Gulf Stream: "The Disappointments of Photography"

Interim: "East Thirtieth Street"

The Lyric: "Word Repository"

Michigan Quarterly Review: "City Market"

Parnassus: "Horsehead Nebula," "Rumination"

Pivot: "On a Footnote in Plato's *Symposium*," "Self-portrait in a Cocked Hat," "Snow Drift"

Poet Lore: "Marble Hill"

Poetry Northwest: "Anaesthesia Green"

Southern Humanities Review: "You Are Perseus, But I Am Not Andromeda"

The Southern Review: "For the Fog Horn When There Is No Fog"

Sou'wester: "Storm Vigil"

Western Humanities Review: "You Furze, Me Gorse"

Contents

As no one point, nor dash,
Which are but accessories to this name,
The showers and tempests can outwash,
So shall all times find me the same;
You this entireness better may fulfill,
Who have the pattern with you still.
　　　　　　　　　—John Donne

1

Eclipse

Every so often I am dilated; the pupils
Swallow everything—a catchall soup,
Two cauldrons, stubborn in the bald glare

Of bathroom light. They are hunting sleep—
The sea grass, the blue cot rocking;
In sleep I am a Spanish dancer,

Awaiting my cue at the velvet curtain,
Now and then groping for the sash,
Or on horseback, abducted, thumping

Through pampas. I sleep too much;
I curl in at midday, sheepish,
In strange rooms. Clouds are hurrying by—

The walls, a wash of white; still my eyes
Are mazing through their dark gardens,
The great lamp shut, the crescents duplicating.

It is only a temporary state of affairs.
The sun boils behind the moon.

Anaesthesia Green

At the forked vein's crux,
The largest on the back of your hand,
The doctor points his needle.
You'll feel a bee sting.
Count backwards from a hundred.
You're going in.

To the sleep bath, the sulfur pail,
The seed pod of the maple.
So many skins and temperatures!
By ninety-eight it still burns
Like a van Gogh window,
Fervent, phosphorescent.

By ninety-three
You are peeling back leaves
In the darkened forest.
You have cooled to lichen, almost
Silver, outspread in the eaves of the bark
Like small arthritic hands.

You comb through the ionic ferns,
The mosses lying like animals.
You drift, cooler still—
The succulents:
Crassula, sedum, sempervivum,
Thick as limbs.

Somewhere in the low thirties
(If you were still counting)
You find yourself inside

A sinking house, peering into the edges
Of an antique mirror.
Deep in the intestines of the glass

You spy a thousand tiny rooms,
Cell after cell full of ether.
The same shiver wakes you
To this iron bed,
At your lips the taste of tin.
This is the coldest you have ever been.

The Disappointments of Photography

I was five years old, in a red and white patchwork.
Poised and grimacing with Olympian effort,
I flung a Slinky at the camera. Unblinking,
My father released the shutter,
One-hundredth of a second
Of light on a toy spring—
A pile of white lines arching from my hand.
The silver rings had gone,
Long fallen. I hunt them now, on all fours,
Through every upright line on the lawn.
The past is a space between grasses, a channel in the loam.
Once I was luminous, I was clicked in and shaking,
My skin a dry plate of open pores,
My dress brighter than Ektachrome.

Street Blind

Past August height, the leaves
    Forget the tree.

Aslant, a moving piebald,
    A fleet of corpuscles—

Stemless shadows
    Of a sun post-solstice,

Disjoined, as when words
    Forget to look

Both ways, atomize, unknit,
    And fall apace,

Deciduous,
    To grays, arcane, strewn,

But nonetheless resigned
    To new reference—

Pavement's impressed permanence—
    Cuneiform, the concrete lawn.

City Market

A round and constant sound persists—
Unpatterned as the fall of tangled waters, it issues

From the ventilation grate beneath
The salad bar, beneath the oiled beans

And trammeled cabbage, across the tiled floor
To the jeweled eyes of the fish

All pointing east on parsley—
A comforting busyness, like someone

Hammering stone in a somnolent town:
The high ring of fracture,

The unceasing impress of one
Elemental substance on another,

The fish on greens and ices swimming
Suddenly in recollection:

A river lined with briar, lit with jewelweed.
Even in this crowded space it eddies,

Like the shiftings of discarded
Plastic bags on pavement,

Skirting and flinging themselves for miles,
Pointing you elsewhere.

Containers

My father had a workshop
In the basement of our house—
A room of ingenious containers
That witnessed the completion
Of other ingenious containers:
A gabled birdhouse, a blue
Under-the-sink cabinet, a child's
Window seat. A room of bevel,
Slat, and dowel, and a crooked
Workbench sprinkled with gray
Dust and lined with yellow cans
Bearing an ancient text: *Chock
Full O'Nuts*, crammed with bolts;
Nailed to the wall, a forest-green
Grid of holes holding hooks holding
Tools: all manner of hammer,
Screwdriver, and saw hanging
Like fish off the board,
Glinting in the trail of swung light
From the strung bulb in that small
Room fallen to disuse, even
Shunned, in the years after
He left, still I continued
To creep down there alone,
Snap on the light, and stare
At all the myriad contrivances—
The bearings and the fasteners,
The rusting jars of unknown solutions.

Snow Drift

I only want to write about a space
Three-inches square, in the picket fence's
Stolid corner, that uncontested crevice
Boasting, suddenly, a jagged occurrence
Of snow, Alp-like, resting on the brief ledge
The wooden crossbeam makes: unlikely cliff,
However wedged, suggesting passage
Beyond lawn and property line, as if
Transgression could be intimately known
Through bold example in miniature,
On familiar ground, a trace of snow blown
On a fence, articulation of a dare:
To realize the route the mountain sees,
The fall to nether—valley, wild trees.

Quincy Quarries, Quincy, Mass.

People swam here once, but mostly fell in, drunk,
On dates, and drowned. Today, the deepest quarry
Drained, you come to peer into the naked bottom,
To scale down the inner walls, spray-paint names,
Or glimpse improbable bodily remains, and so

Your reckless beau scrambles precipices ahead
Without question, as if walking to the mailbox,
Pauses by the secret fissure in the padlocked chain-link
Fence, waits for you to arrive, to lie down prone,
And peels back the twisted steel edges, holds them

At bay, and drags you under into the restricted zone:
Patrol car, votive candle, a clutch of mums—
Wilted, white, beside a laminated sign: *$5000*
Reward for Information Regarding _____, *Mother*
Of Three, Missing Since...; the rest you cannot stop

To read, for he has already sped up the cliff
And calls back, faintly, annoyed—"y'allright?"—
Until you manage, gravel-stung and dusty, to the ledge,
The promised vista. Down sixty feet of rusted depths
You discern the more substantial discards: yellow

Chevy, blue Camaro, kitchen sink amidst a scattering
Of hundreds of thin wooden planks, spilled like matchsticks,
From an abandoned attempt at a footbridge. He pops
One Schlitz, and then another. *So this is how they went,*
You think—drunk, in sharpening lust—caress, climax,

Up and over, never found, "Gone missing." At once
The phrase seems oddly active, as if they walked, or ran,

11

Or swam deliberately, efficiently, toward the goal,
The fulfillment of missing, like fishing or shopping
Or out for a drive. You turn. His lips are full and flush,

And as you fumble underneath his faded baseball shirt that same
Delicious smell obliterates the outside air of stain:
His clothes, always surprisingly clean—a bright
Scent, almost orange, with a trace, just beyond
The cotton weave, of morning reefer. He springs

Your bra free, really a redundancy,
You reckon—"Gone missing," that is, like saying
They have gone gone, unloosed, loosed, gone lost,
Tumbled down—like locals falling in, one after
Another, friends of friends, the same way, although

They knew how it could happen, and then he says
Your name, helplessly, and photograph and sign
Are jettisoned from mind, gone, gone, and he says
Your name again, relentless as the cadence sprayed in red
Across the northernmost rock face:

Fuck Beth. Jane Gives Good Head.

Marble Hill

You've missed the train—
The birds care nothing about it.
In the brush, in the eaves of rock
Yellow moths wink like paper.
You've missed the train,
A perfect miss; it snaked by slowly
As you stumbled down the steps from the subway overpass.
Starlings rattle in the brush.
A dayliner passes, puffing clouds in silence.
Maybe you should have married
That rock guitarist from Jersey.
There was a pleasant stillness then—
A home, yellow flutterings—
Which you cannot help considering, bound,
For another hour, to this stubborn plain
While the afternoon sun makes water of the air
And concrete, and in this heat
Edges blur between outcroppings:
Sooted cliffs, car mufflers, non-refundables.
You're getting older;
You're less able to contain your questions.

Is there any marble in this hill at all?

The Colors Are Off This Season

I don't want any more of this mumble—
Orange fireside hues,
Fading sun, autumnal tumble,
Stricken, inimitable—Rose.

I want Pink, unthinking, true.
Foam pink, cream and coddle,
Miniskirt, Lolita, pompom, tutu,
Milkshake. Pink without the mottle

Or the dying fall. Pink adored, a thrall
So pale it's practically white.
A tinted room beneath a gable—
Ice pink, powder, feather-light—

Untried corner of the treble.
I want the lift, not the lower.
Bloodless pink stalled at girl,
No weight, no care, no hour.

Cicatrix

A white blur of absence,
A row of bent crosses.

A trifle—
The eye of a bean!

The orange sits on the table—
An orbit of pores,

A galaxy. It wears its green
Scar like a crown

Beneath the moon
Who follows children

Because she has none.
The fruit,

The red fruit
That wants to fall—

I am that one.

Apology for Sleeping Late

You've done it again—slept
Yourself to obsolescence, slept
Yourself to Rotterdam on that slow
Velveted train, that impossibly expensive
Disorient Express, not express at all, circuitous,

Digressing inexplicably to Flanders,
Past phalanx and loggia, paroxysm and
Quiescence; you've quaffed a pint of absinthe
Handed you by lackeys, washed it down with capers;
Night-sweated through your skivvies into Dordrecht

Where train transmogrified
To streetcar bearing signs for Rice-a-Roni,
And you thought yourself in Frisco, which meant
You gained three hours, so you slept on as streetcar
Flattened to canoe and skimmed through waters Delftly.

Tomorrow you will try anew.
Armed with rectitude, regret, alarmed
And freshly brewed, you will arise, atone,
Untorque, shut bedroom door and strap yourself
To straight-backed chairs of wood from noble trees.

No guarantee. It's not a trifle
To secure the pallid temple from the soak
Of narcotic tides, the throng of weeds encroaching
On the border. Which is all by way of saying you'll
Probably do it again—sleep through post and telephone,

And although there's not
A milkman to be missed, you will sleep
Through the milk's drinkability. In your defense,
You've been busy in the route; as you retrace the round,
It deepens, makes its layers known—profound, Pleistocene.

The things you've done in dreams—a life! Low Country.

East Thirtieth Street

for V. Condello

It's nightfall on your street, appointed time.
In this over-quiet part of town
Doorways spook: a brownstone without number,

Vacant, announced by two imitation
Gas lamps burning day and evening through,
As if conversing, other to the one.

I slink from Third to Second Avenue.
A wall-eyed china bulldog glares past glaze
And antique glass from a crowded window.

East, I go and go, pausing at the blazon,
"Marchi," that blinks behind ivy and maroon-
Vested men with arms crossed, counting down

To First: your lobby, chandelier and indoor tree.
You, the interlocutor, would ask me
Why I'm crying over light bulbs. I'd say

There's something ominously binary,
A silent pattern: one and nothing.
You'd ask me. You have answered. Gone.

The postulated future's past;
The hour's done;
There's nothing here but water.

Storm Vigil

Minutes before rain I stood by the wide road.
Above the lawns and violet pavement
The clouds hung like a false ceiling,
The air too sulfurous for traffic.
It was turbid in the briar;
The grass blades silvered,
The black spruce was bristling.
I peered into the leaf, into the quick
Sprigs and bent figure-eights, for a sign.
Then, in the needles of the narrow pine,
There came a twitch. The tree's seismograph.
I waited until it couldn't get darker.

Greenwich Mean Time

A storm swathes the Atlantic coast:
Heavy Snow, Blowing Snow; Ceiling Low; Dewpoint Twenty.
The Capes, those lonely outposts,
Are summoned like deities: *May, Cod, Hatteras,*
Waters green and roiling,
Roads slung with blown fences.
On a blue map by an excited meteorologist
A repeating three-frame sequence
Approximates the storm's progress:
A swollen white spiral curling inward,
Culminating in an unmistakable
Plumed horse head centered on Virginia.

Meanwhile, in London: showers.
The Royal Observatory.
It comforts me to think of it:
A round-the-clock staff
Of most reliable persons.
A room of compass and chronometer,
Green radar screens. At each display
A line sweeps, someone broods—
Checking, counterchecking:
Seconds-to-the-minute, tides,
Earth's alignment.
I'm no longer afraid to relinquish the worry
Although without such a weight
I may be flattened by a breeze,
Laid out prone, pressed east-west
In a dress—sea-green,
Prime meridian.
Oh, my Greenwich Mean.
Zero Longitude!

2

Destroying Angel (Amanita virosa)

I'm way in, way in you, Mushroom—
Membered in your harem,
Shirted in your morning veil,
An eager moth at your light,
Your curtained lumens,
All laid out in bridal white.

How did you come to be—
Hatted and ruffled,
Fait accompli?
I was studious, at peace;
I was minding my own business.
You thumbed right up and nudged me.

It was dawn. The leaves,
The intractable roots of trees,
Gave way; the violets stood
And watched. I tripped and fell.
I am still falling.

This species, like many others,
Can grow to sizes far exceeding the normal range.
You don't need me;
You reseed easy as winking.
The circles loosen and descend,
Pale rings that shudder into powder,

Sifting through the forest floor,
Gaining footholds in the light rain,
Thrones of betrothal accruing,
Until I am enveloped—eloped

In a one-way promise, bespoken by a spore,
No time for a proper wedding—

A quick note posted home,
"Am sluggish, having visions":
The snails are hungry and thronging;
Everyone wants a piece.

Rumination

Were my mouth to find yours in the gloom
Of dying promises—canted, mid-sentence,
Mid-phrase or quotation—were I on a lark
To marry wood, the hard pine panels
Of this room, your lips, the rivulet
Tips of your lingering sweats,
Who would I be then?

Were your mouth to find mine in the half-dark,
In the overhang of cloud, by the skulls,
Amidst the risen hairs, the certain volts
Of concupiscence—what would I become?
An afternoon, a row of trees, a route
Already known: now sloping, now climbing in the distance,
A wide road, slick with rain—

Do Not Touch Me, I Am Caesar's

The fast hind's lust—I wonder if you know.
Aging cowboy, boasting over ale
Of pretties knocked up by your arrow,
Of tress and tendon pinned down by your skill.
I wonder if you know how I can carve
You out in well-placed blows of hoof to bone;
I wonder if you know how velvets burn
And chafe beneath the collar, in the grove.
They say I'm marked for centuries, penned
To the nines, the end of time, the emperor.
I wonder if you know the hind's a whore.
You circle, point. I should run, but relent
With your approach—your strokes, your begging head.
My bond is null, my lauded god long dead.

Lethe

I've hit bottom now—your murky water.
Too breathless to swim, too freighted to float,
I sank from light and shore, my dress wrapped strait
Around my limbs, preventing any stir.
And this is how you thrive, consummate host,
Coaxing reeds from your edges, roots from soil,
Now sparkling in conquest, now misted and still,
But not inert, planning tributary, tryst.
There must be a way out (not how I came),
But if I knew, I forgot in the lace
Of your currents, in the deep chills that numb,
In your muddy lips' promise: *Drink. No blame.*
What sweet obliterations bloom in a kiss—
Morphines, poppies, plums.

You Are Perseus, But I Am Not Andromeda

To begin, I'm pale but not that pretty,
Tied and sad at times, but not completely
Helpless, although my circumstance alarms;
Parents mill about, waving their arms.
You know you could win them over; you dove
Down and won me. Half-drowning I was reedy:
A clutch of swaying tendrils in the sea.
I was softened in that silty cove,
Blindly feeding, green and pliable.
Then I rose for air, and there, like coral,
I changed my disposition. I'm the muse
But not the maiden—yours, but not the prize,
Fresh and chaste and dowried, you think you're due.
I'm the jagged rock you cling to.

The Comet Is Worn Out by the Sun

Don't ask this speeding, icy ball of offal
To make another trip around; you ruin
Me each orbit, each closing circle
Hastens me to dust—disintegration.
It bores me now, this ritual of flight,
Though I'll admit that I enjoyed it once:
The reckless spin of my reflected light
Across your vaporous circumference.
Don't count the hours in a sulky boil,
Anticipating grace—this comet has quit,
Has carried your dross in its limp, dusty tail,
Hybrid of friction and angst, on a course cursed
From inception. No sense clinging to it;
The answer is annihilation. You first.

You Furze, Me Gorse

The only true synonyms in the English language are "furze" and "gorse."
— Tennyson

Furze, Gorse, of equal and abiding value
But for the speed of each word off the lips:
The warm and cornucopic cup of U
Hanging on by the very fingertips
Of the lazy Z. Furze, you would lie,
Luxurious; you would make a mattress;
You would carry yellow torches nightly,
Barbed fingers circling in slow caress.
Raise the lamps high, let us look at ourselves:
Once a tender union, now turned fierce,
Twins scratching across sands and rocky shelves.
Furze, Gorse. Which cuts worse?
The claws that grab and cling, purpling the skin,
Or the sudden spike that stabs and runs?

Word Repository

Eloped somewhere on the periphery—
Our progeny—quibbles, clips, and barbs,
All the words we've said, those still-lying shards,
Shorn from sentence, emptied of story,
Pointed fragments in a deep steel drawer
Slammed shut in a vault and bolted.
They might catch the light if light permitted—
Those half-formed, whispered plans we swore
We'd not lay bare. Discovered, on release
They'd quickly rise without a backward glance—
Newborn, no longer belonging to us.
And now I think they were the glinting core
And we two the mute appurtenance:
Bodies wrapped in blankness, nothing more.

Manhattan, 5 a.m.

Night wrings out its final summer
Sweats, the evening's discards:

Green chewing gums pooled and flattened,
A pair of men's briefs in a bundle,

Soaked perhaps, steaming on a subway grating.
A *Times'* Late Edition title skips along

The pavement, sounds the cracks:
"Free and Confused by Infinite Possibility."

It is not summer rain that beats at each temple,
And who says a new day washes us clean?

My fingers tremble. A cab obligingly
Arrives—north, northeast—Broadway

Sinks and rallies. At a summit I think I see
Connecticut, I think I know Connecticut—

Verdant tinge above the metal girdage, until,
Deposited stoop side, I realize I've skipped

From night to day and bypassed dawn;
The neighborhood rooster calls,

Always late. Somewhere else it was decried
By birds, so loudly I couldn't wander

Past it; windows rattled, sun razored
Through wet grass, and clover shook,

Anticipating bees. Somewhere else I had
To notice; there was fanfare and brigade, a litany

Of fowl, and not this lonely cock,
Twitching and strutting by a gated pane,

Spending himself for an alley.

"Veritable Strasbourg"

Face-down in a pitcher: "Fischer"—
A blonde boy, too young to drink,
In knickers kicking atop a keg
Under a fair sky
In a field of blackberries.

I had not been, truly, and I wanted:
Veering off—over seas,
Rocking in a tiny skiff,
A series of midnights strung
And billowing like flimsy paper lanterns,

Swinging orbs in lambent rows
Like bottles gleaming, backlit, in the bar:
Beauties! Amber, blush, and Curacao,
Galliano monolith, green gem,
And my face, of like color, agreeing

In the mirror, fashionably starved,
Across waters lapping, sleepless.
I might have done—gone on
And kept on going, truly, another year,
Could I have lived that long,

Had it not been for the interstices,
Sudden, somber, dry—
The depths outplumbed,
The thin boat run aground
Against a damning silence.

The Watchman

I know a lighthouse, a man sometimes:
All turning eye and stem, source and line,

Gyring on through drought and squall
And fogs of varied countenance, a ray

That slants and rounds, portending ground
Or at the very least location for some

Nubile civilian who jaunts beyond the narrow walk
And finds herself in midnight waters. He circles

Twice and stalls on pale skin—light meets
Light—they gleam. He doesn't know until

She passes that his purpose lay therein—
Not in the solemn furtherance of grand armadas,

But in the saltatory capers of fair and hapless
Plankton. So he waits, decades hence, for her

Return, revisiting the same circumference,
Seeking a center; anxious, insomniacal, he probes

Each barren crest, each foamy mane, and peers
Into the bottom, though centuries elapse without a sign,

Because it is his nature to fixate and mine, because
He is a creature of hope.

Run, Don't Walk

Because you know that not even the dictate
Of a shuffling song in 4/4 can carve
A proper course out of the arching surf
Enfolding you, that green wave thick with bait
And rank with disinhibiting toxins
Amplifying itself every hour;
Because you know you lack the stature,
Countermand, and balance to ride it in;
Run, when a certain body comes around;
Leave the party early; don't wash dishes;
Don't wait until it crashes and you're eating sand
In undertow; just go, i.e., egress
Whichever way—by cab, on foot or crutch.
Because you've changed, but you haven't changed that much.

The Dark Bookcases

You are tired of the dark bookcases—
Stained them yourself, did a lousy job;
Stain-and-polyurethane-in-one tends to drip in knobs
That fix over the bright, uneven paperbacks
From college, some of which you never read

But nonetheless boxed and moved and unpacked for years:
Twenty-three boxes of books
And these two colossal bookcases,
Which are really only poor imitations of
The original dark bookcases

From the dining room in the house where you grew up—
That elaborate library with the curling iron lamps,
The leaded casement windows, the Persian carpet lit
With birds—where you sat when you were three
And tugged at the books and threw them on the floor

So your parents moved all the cheap novels
To the lower shelves, until you were eight
And could stand up easily, and you pushed the books
All the way in against the wall, while the floors rang
With the shifting wood, until you grew into a teenager

And just stood—silent, staring for hours, the print
Turned cipher, the 1950's Faulkners
Dressed up like Harlequin romances,
The Modern Library Man always running,
Fleet and silver,

Through the spines' midnight, in that house
On the highest point of land on the street.
The house burned and you don't have those books
But you remember them,
Their strange titles like incantations through the years:

The Proud Tower
Pale Horse, Pale Rider
Time and Again
An End to Dying

Peregrine

A firm grey slant in even sunlight,
    A shadow on the rolling copper cornice
        Of the observatory roof delays me, then

Takes flight—
    A blade in a sky indolent with gasses.
        He leaves tidings in the evergreen,

Strange and bloodless:
    A pair of pigeon wings, the joints picked clean,
        The flight feathers intact,

Transferable—a dissembling lattice
    Of silk hook and filament. I scan
        The air, adrift from numbness for a moment,

My head in full pivot,
    My eyes obsidian.
        What will it mean to be as solitary as this?

The Loud Lament of Disconsolate Chimera

I am wafted by the loss of men, a flume
Of wind through alleys, wafted, paper-thin,
A slip of missive from a bedroom

Dresser, flung and flipping past the iron
Windows, circling in the inner courts
Of condominiums, glancing on uniform

Terraces, plotted trees, cinderblock balconies,
To airshafts where rosetted birthday cakes
Implode before they hit the bottom.

I am driven by the dross of dead connections:
Senseless thrum of double line and dash
At night down highways south to Newport

As I passed my late teens belted in a snazzy
Mazda, fleeing from that hum that clung beneath
The axle of the car and desisted only briefly

In that town athrong with Oxford-shirted,
Khakied tourists, where I was fed, unfolded,
Quickened home, well past curfew; it returned,

Persisted down my street, through bolted door,
Dark house; partner of my dread, it bore me
Up when I was banished, sentenced to itinerancy

For too much itinerancy. It whistled at my back,
My bag crammed with necessity; it waited as
I scrubbed my body—hand soap in public

Restrooms); it winged through city streets
And courthouses crowded with papers
Of divorce; it lingered and reshuffled them,

And reckoned me "THE CHILD"—*YOU, YOU,*
Most stridently on Sunday afternoons, ending visits
With my father, out of time in the custodial shuffle;

It sounded in the elevators, shook the steel doors
And skirted round the orange hall, through the smell
Of neighbors' broiling steaks, through the falsely

Sunny yellow kitchen, past the Naugahyde recliner;
It fretted in an *O*, or, lower, a demonic *M*,
It lingered at the windows, worsened, blew

Dirges in their cracks, and their steel frames
Did not gird them against it; it hummed and cooed
And taunted them, bade them *jettison, soon, soon.*

Decades since, another city, it reenters variously
Down the halls of brand-new complexes; it circles
In blue waiting rooms, and reinvents itself as wind

Canned in gray containers, noise for noise's sake,
Plangent, mortuary, but veering, ineluctably,
Toward syntax; it hunts past voice, seeks a sentence,

Vies for words—those dears, they burgeon,
Age, and die, and never quite make sense;
I watch them fly, askance, and I am wafted

By them, I am wafted by the loss of men,
The press of wind in empty spaces.

3

In the Cellar, Dreaming

You palm the cool concrete floor,
As late snows trace the bare
Stems of ivies at the window wells,
And you lie supine,
Smelling earth, and your gaze
Drifts lazily across several
Exquisite finger paintings
Executed in childhood—
Unintentional seascapes of eel,
Urchin, coral in full flower—
Stapled to the crumbling wall amid
The complacent hum of the stout
Teutonic boiler, circa 1927,
Boasting elegant archaic signage:
When arrow falls below
Zero, add water. Asterisks
Of dusts drift past, boards
Groan and shift on boards
And still you lie there still,
Like an invalid, as larvae
Of potential flying things foment,
One twitching chrysalis
After another, in the dark slant
Space of the bulkhead, unaware
Of what they're waiting for—
Seedtime—
The brown doors thrown open
Into wings.

"Sally Go Round the Roses"

She swears she will not think about it—
How the hot street slopes, and her thin dress
Pulls and puckers—how the air
Almost gropes, full of glances.

How the street slopes inevitably downward.
A man whistles, a low horn honks.
Why does she walk so loud?
The eye-hook at the nape of the neck,

The shifting fabric, the high sandals.
Her heels on the concrete feel like an event.
And so she hurries.
Sally go round the roses.

A stranger calls out—
She will not think of it—
She will think instead about the song:
Last night, on low in her room, in the tape deck

With the two lit windows, two needles wagging,
Almost weightless, between the black and red.
The Jaynetts—four girls in the Bronx
Leaning toward a silver microphone.

She can hear them breathing,
And she can hear them holding back,
And when they let it go they send the needles soaring
Far into the red range in the window of intensity—

Sally baby cry, let your hair hang down.
She crosses the street. The eye-hooks!
The air is hot and close, a tincture,
Like the current at the center
Of the palest flower—trapped light in cool petals,
Found pink at the core.

It is only reflection. There is nothing really there...

Sally, go round
And though it is itself a method of elision,
She still feels strangely folded out of harm.

The Linen Closet

Oh, the linen closet, imperial
Ladder of shelves, gold towels glowing
With repose, night creams pearled, in pots,
Their risen oils yellowed at the rims,
Tubed salves, perfumed proteins.

Tall and narrow, narrow and deep,
The linen closet of worry and care!
On the highest shelves, the recondite liquids
In brown, bottled sternly: Peroxide,
Witch Hazel, and the dread purgative,

Ipecac. You might have died or been renewed,
Clavicles dewed by that arched-back soap,
Inimitably scented, cuts bridged by red
Tinctures, muscles slackened in the heating pad's
Green mosses. But no matter the potion

You could not ignore the space
At the back, the absolute black
In the bowels of the shelves, beyond the patch
And blanch of gauze, the catch of clots—
That unflagging question (past cure)

No tonic or robe could appease,
No meter or prodding inspection
Could probe—you could not quite make it out,
And you would not forget it.

Note to Self

I was waiting for forecasts from Swansea,
For developments in prints, clear rubrics
Unperceived in the act of photography,
Some pattern in a flash of sun against
A second-story window in a row of flats
In Hackney district—
I was waiting for a map in clear Queen's
English, lines articulated by skilled
And steady hands,
Proper nouns declining certain ways.

Now I think they are trees,
And the map is in my hand.
It is my hand, just pointing east,
This side of the Atlantic,
One cricket pulsing under reeds
Well past his season. When he stops
I write it, Note to self: *Return, address.*
Note to self: *Come see me.*
Write it out in pokeweed juice,
Post it from a country mailbox
Along a crabbed embankment,
A riverway still turning darkly.
A home without a house,
A zip code lost in hemlocks.

Niantic

I always say, it must give way, it must all pass on
Soon, the husks, the frayed leaves clung to ossified sticks,
Illuminated by a flash of tedium: sleek
Silver Amtrak where I sit, a slow boxy stasis,
Shuttling endlessly between the same two terminals—
Boston, New York, New York, Boston —until it is no
Longer clear to me which was origin and which is
Destination, and maybe origin is after
All and destination was, and where the hell does one
Reside, in shrub and tree—leaf fall loaming into roots?
And then suddenly, a coastal town, I never know
Exactly when, but somewhere in the middle—a bay,
Egrets alighting, and then cows, and twists of briar,
And one gigantic trunk, long dead, full of green shoots.

City Hall Station, IRT

A hum arrives: low wind in a row
Of thinning trees, high but sinking

Scale of an engine overhead some evening
As you speculate alone on your front stoop

Before brownstone roofs assembling,
Or, late at night, below ground, a rattle, antecedent

In the tracks, of a train that fast approaches
En route to a station condemned to disuse

For its perilous gap between platform and car.
And because you ask politely

They allow you to remain throughout the turn,
Through the vaulted passage to the green

Tile sacristy, unpeopled, somehow gleaming still
Among extinguished chandeliers, echoing

With the train's intrusion, or is that pulse
Your own, most audible in vacancy, before

The line ends and reverses, most free
When most alone, just you and the motorman,

And he has closed his door.

Aster Hill

At the end of the dead end street:
A brief wood, a field of asters,
Yellow, purple, white, dotting the quick grass

Up the slope
To the row of birches
At the edge of the wood.

In the half-dark, under the cover
Of oaks, the ground simmered
With mosses, with faint paths

Parting for the spathes
Of skunk cabbage,
The broad leaves,

The slow heat of it breathing.
Plowed now, all of it,
Unmapped.

I imagine it still
In the late hours:
The grasses have cooled,

The briar is spiralling.
The ray flowers
Glint and collide,

They fix on points,
They mirror the constellations—
Lights from a source long expired,

Persisting through atmospheres.

Lunar Landing

A step away,
Earth, humid entanglements.

A foot set down:
A work-in-progress

On a dry surface,
A text of treads bowed

Slightly by the human arch,
Toe shadowed. The sense

Cannot be reckoned—
Between where you are

And where you were—
The avoirdupois difference

Between the emblem
And the thing that made it,

The extension
Of a body in a state

Of compromised magnetics:
Disencumbered,

Skipping on granules, in
sun—
Another angle altogether.

Cassetta Frame (Italy, circa 1600)
Robert Lehmann Collection, Metropolitan Museum of Art

I wonder what his hands were like—skin,
Thumbprint's orbits, half moon of the nail—
The artisan who plied bough and alloy, chisel,
Stone, for the sake of circumscription:
Poplar, walnut, ebony, pear, niello,
Crystal, lapis. The words abscond from wood
And bloom in trees: Pioppo tremulo;
Forma di pera. I confess to find
Myself astonished by outskirts of things:
Hem and shirr, ice storm, sea coast, shadow, fringe,
To find myself forsworn to the mixture,
Poplar, walnut, ebony, pear,
Niello, crystal, lapis. Lapse! No life
But in the rim; no word but on the lips.

Note: The materials used in the frame were typed out on a small index card
beneath the frame on display.

Self-portrait in a Cocked Hat
(Francisco Goya, circa 1790-1792)

The coat is a river, the hat a dark mountain.
The grim face between insinuates in stipple:
It knows the disjuncture inscribed in the pattern.

Through hatch and cross-hatch the gestures return;
They weave a lapel, and in shadows redouble.
The coat is a river, the hat a dark mountain.

Black footpaths—mind's triangulated crown—
Full of tempers, delight and despair each in spell;
It knows the disjuncture inscribed in the pattern.

Confession brokered in brown ink and pen,
Lips firmly set against a landscape of trouble.
The coat is a river, the hat a dark mountain

Whose outlines succumb to the strain
Between lived and made, as if to say the battle's
Been lost, disjuncture declaring the pattern

In progressive collision of lines—
A mirror—your river and mountain and fall,
The turn in the pattern, the yoke of disjuncture,
The skill of admitting the flaw.

A Low Fence Made in a Particular Way

Let us say we had space but lacked latitude—

    We had herbage but lacked verdure, lacked the true
Green colloquy, the core (rolling in grass, sprig-

    Like, tendrils ourselves); we had oak and hemlock
But lacked stature, the trunks' undeniable

    Presence; we had wood but lacked will. Water turned
The wheel of the mill, voices seeking echoes

    Resounded from embankment to embankment,
That same old sun ventured up over the hill,

    And we stood there simply watching. Let us say
We had fixation but lacked concentration—

    We didn't need so many terraces.
So from this line of demarcation on

    We'll endeavor a region, not so large, not
Nearly so dear, a lawn lit with fruit trees,

    Gnarled perhaps, even blighted sometimes, but
Purposeful; we'll endeavor a space and fence

    It slightly—mortise, tenon—a low fence made
In a particular way, to remind us

    Of the edges, sing their praises in perennials,
And cross them.

On a Footnote in Plato's *Symposium*[1]

I suppose we're mad for loving footnotes—
The promise stowed in a tiny number
Proudly flagging the quotation
"To lay up glory immortal forever"—
And in the drive past text to precipice,
We plummeted past pulp and typeface,
Seeking a source, a proprietor at bottom,
But instead found only "A line of poetry
Of unknown origin," and in chagrin
Convinced ourselves we knew—
At least that it was human, and didn't someone
Of that fellow race say something once
About dust, vis à vis issuance and return—
But when, exactly, where? And that chap gone
Unnamed as well, laid up forever
In his own annotation; we sought him
At that shore, below the legible horizon;
We dug through cool leaves of like color,
And of nothing found we knew a bit more.

1 Trans. Alexander Nehamas and Paul Woodruff (Indianapolis, 1989), p. 55.

After the Long Chard Season
"My salad days, when I was green in judgment…"
　　　　　　　　　　　　　—Antony and Cleopatra

After the long chard season
We had a lot of chard.
Winter ran for miles—stone
Fortress, struck leaves, frozen yard.
Even the dirt was dead.

But we had chard—abundant bundles.
Forty days in snow drifts, eating stalks.
Eighty days, a stockpot, stirring.
And then an easing of bombardment,
A grocer rushing down a busy street,
Purposely, solemnly, carrying chervil—
Charein, from the Greek, *to take pleasure in.*

Who knew there were so many greens?
Chive grass, Boston lettuce pollard,
Elysian shade of parsley boughs.
It might just possibly be true
That all that was undone is through.
These are the salad days.
These are the salad days!

Horsehead Nebula

The blacksmith knows the iron
Word for horse, knows the aquiline
Musculature of the features,
How the idea of eyes ignited
In the fire, and the mane swam
In articulations of the mold, knows
The liquid inception and the end—
The stamp and final ring of absolute
Ferrosity. Knows how the dark head
Bides the red country house,
How round post marries ground,
Knows anatomy and root: forelock
And throatlatch, *equus, hross, hrata,*

Horsehead Nebula.
Black quiz on the red horizon.
His brood of stars nearby,
He watches, silent, wakeful,
A collusion of gasses in profile:
Slow grace of the head, sweep
Of the long nose, curve of neck,
Unseen for centuries but intuited
On lawns, alone, in mote and shadow,
At light's collapse and gallop's ceasing,
When dusts combine, the figure—
The unperceived persistence
In the backward space of things—
The air behind the air.

Star-nosed Mole *(Condylura cristata)*

It seems burdensome at times,
A hindrance, a "despite,"

This fleshy protuberance
That bumps and flails,

Appended coelenterate,
All edges, all feeling,

An unasked-for inheritance,
A fluke in DNA.

Sometimes you think
It has nothing to do whatsoever

With your self proper, the proper self
You've pulled, propelled, and pronounced

Out of the earth; it gets in the way
(Dark loam tunnel)

Of the way (winding river),
As if there were two,

And arrival were anything other
Than what is right in front of you.

For the Fog Horn When There Is No Fog

Still sounding in full sun past the jetty,
While low tide waves lap trinkets at your feet,

And you skip across the drying trails,
Fling weeds, and don't think anything of worry.

For the horn that blares even as you call it stubborn,
In error, out of place. For the ridicule endured,

And the continuance.
You can count out your beloved—crustaceans—

Winking in the spray, still breathing in the wake,
Below the hooking flights of gulls,

Through the horn's threnody.
Count them now among the moving. They are.

For weathervane and almanac, ephemeris and augur,
Blameless seer versed in bones, entrails, landed shells;

For everything that tries to counsel vigilance—
The surly sullen bell, before the going,

The warning that reiterates across
The water: there might be fog someday

(They will be lost), there might be fog
And even squall, and you'll have nothing

But remembrance, and you will have to learn
To be grateful.